Dedication

Dedicated to the many suffragists and abolitionists who worked tirelessly for the furtherance of human rights and dignity. Many received little or no credit for their efforts. We are all indebted to them.

Acknowledgements

I would like to express my deep appreciation to Dr. Carol Steinhagen for sharing her expertise on Frances Dana Barker Gage; to Linda Showalter for aiding me in utilizing the resources of the Marietta College Special Collections; to Kelly Lincoln for allowing me to visit the Barker homestead and to Galen Finley for making a visit to Mount Airy possible; to my editor, Dr. Marybeth Peebles, for her constant support and guidance; and, finally, to the illustrator, Emily Bonnette Hendershot, my heartfelt gratitude for providing the lens through which these letters are seen.

\- C.M.

My gratitude goes to Cathy Mowrer, the author, for having patience and trust in me to carry out her vision of paying tribute to Frances Dana Barker Gage; to Kelly Lincoln for sharing the Barker homestead and her artistry she's found there; and to my husband Mark for his beautiful guitar tunes and encouragement.

\- E.B.H.

Preface

Born to one of the earliest pioneer families to settle in the Ohio territory, Frances Dana Barker was born on October 12, 1808 at Wiseman's Bottom outside of Marietta, Ohio. Her parents, Colonel Joseph and Elizabeth Dana Barker had traveled from Massachusetts to Marietta with Elizabeth's parents, Captain William and Mary Bancroft Dana. Grandmother Dana was an outspoken abolitionist and is purported to have helped slaves escape through the Underground Railroad system in southeastern Ohio. It is in these background experiences that we see the beginning of what would drive Frances Dana Barker Gage to become an extremely influential woman in the reform movements of the 19th century.

Frances D. Gage's work as an abolitionist, suffragist, and temperance advocate speaks of her commitment to humanitarian causes. In addition, she also dedicated time toward educating freed slaves, providing aid to soldiers during the Civil War, and authoring three temperance novels as well as countless newspaper and journal articles. She served as presiding officer at many reform-minded conventions, speaking at most. Notwithstanding this busy schedule, Frances always made time for her beloved husband and eight children.

Frances Gage was well known in the literary realm as Aunt Fanny. She used this endearing name in her freelance writing, books of poetry, and her three novels. Frances was often introduced at meetings and conventions as Aunt Fanny as well. In the *Ohio Cultivator* and other reform-minded periodicals, Aunt Fanny wrote "letters" to her readers. Feeling a connection with her approachable style, they came to trust her and rely upon her advice.

I have chosen to use Fanny's "letters" to chronicle important events in the life of this amazing woman who fought for the rights of women and freedom for slaves in 19th century America. While the information included in the letters is true, taken from many different sources including the memoirs of her sister Catharine Barker, the words are my own and not from the pen of Fanny. But, thanks to the many letters, speeches, and anecdotes from Frances Dana Barker Gage herself, I had much to choose from.

Frances D. Gage did not garner and sustain the attention that several of her fellow activists did as the 20th century approached. Indeed, she is often merely a footnote in the history of American reform movements. Frances was not one to seek recognition for herself but rather for the causes that she so relentlessly advocated for. She saw herself as the carrier of words that might influence others to action. Perhaps she said it best in an article written for the *Ohio Cultivator* in 1852 when she compared her words to seeds that could flourish if planted in the warmth of a human heart.

"So I dropped my tiny seed and when I had finished my work I sat down to rest, and with the point of this tiny pen, I fling my thoughts to the world. May they be good seed planted in the right season." Aunt Fanny

Grandmother Dana

Wiseman's Bottom • October, 1817

Dearest Grandmother Dana,

I hope your trip home to Belpre went well. My sisters complain that riding a barge 12 miles down the Ohio River is grueling. I rather enjoyed my last visit to your farm and suspect that you enjoy making the trip as well.

I am actually writing this letter to apologize for any ill behavior I demonstrated while you were staying with us. Truly, I think Catharine exaggerates too much about my lack of interest in helping with the dishes. There are other chores I could be of more help with. I'm strong and enjoy the outdoors. Do you remember this past winter when most of the family were too sick to work? I took it upon myself to keep the farm animals fed and watered. Axe in hand, I chopped through a foot of ice to get creek water to 40 or 50 head of cattle and horses. Isn't that of more value than washing pots? Well, I'm sorry that you had to hear the tattling of Mary and Catharine. "Tut tut", as you always say.

I do have news that I think will make you quite proud of me. I have come up with an idea to make my own money. The Frenchman who boards with us is in need of apple seeds and offered 50¢ for a quart. I picked out all the seeds left over from the ground-up apples Father used in cider and soon had 50¢ worth of silver in my hand. I sent it with our bound boy Dan, who was going to Marietta the next day, with directions to spend it all on foolscap paper. Now I can retreat to my special writing place that Father calls my sanctum and write to my heart's content. Oh, you'll be hearing more from me, Grandmother. Until next time, tut, tut.

Your Loving Granddaughter,

Fanny

Note: Bound children were often placed with respectable families during this time period in order to provide them with a skill and/or education.

Brother Luther

Wiseman's Bottom • May, 1818

Dearest Brother Luther,

This letter comes to you from a confused younger sister seeking your advice. I have looked to you for help so many times whilst you were still at home and then away at college in Athens. I still need your guidance, even now, though I am almost ten years old.

I have been doing well in my studies and getting all my lessons done. I'm even ahead of Catharine and many others at our small log school. But I don't think the teacher likes me. He is always calling me a mischief-maker and sometimes makes me stand with my hands out level while he hits them with a flat piece of board. It stings and brings tears to my eyes, but I don't cry in front of him or the other pupils.

Yesterday, I turned in one of my best compositions. It was hard to read but all of my thoughts were down just as I was thinking them. The schoolmaster accused me of borrowing the ideas because he doesn't think I'm smart enough to think of them myself. I was so hurt and angry. Catharine and even little Charlotte tried to stand up for me and assure him that I wrote the paper. He handed it back to me and moved on to teaching arithmetic. I still don't think he believes me. I'll show him someday that my head isn't full of rocks.

Oh, dear brother, I miss you. Do you see your friend Thomas Ewing very often? I've heard gossip that you are both sweet on pretty Maria Devol. I've also seen their initials carved in that large beech tree down by the river. I hope you win in this contest. I might like Thomas for my own beau one day. I guess it's true what Catharine says about me – I'm a "young colt let loose."

Your Devoted Sister,

Fanny

Grandmother Dana

Wiseman's Bottom • June, 1823

Dear Grandmother,

I received your letter today. Thank you for inviting me to spend the rest of the summer with you. I've already spoken with Mother and Father and they agree that time spent with you is always worthwhile. I've been working on a sampler that I'm anxious for you to see as well as some new calico dresses I sewed together this past winter.

Father tells me to let you know that I will be there after July 4th. You know how much he loves attending the festivities in Marietta. I don't think any event will ever top the one several years ago in which he gave the celebratory speech. People still mention his creative poem titled *The Birthday of Uncle Sam*. I've been writing poetry too. I'll bring some favorites to share with you.

I must confess to you that I'm a bit nervous about traveling by one of the great plantations on my way to your home. Catharine and I passed by there on one of our trips to see Betsy and her husband Rufus. We heard great cries and moans coming from the Virginia side of the river. As our barge drew closer, we could see several boats loaded with slaves that were headed south to be sold at auction. We were told that the slave owner needed the money to pay off debts. It was horrific to see families separated, some standing on the embankment calling out for their loved ones. Those on the boats had shackles around their ankles. Catharine called out, "Oh, if this is slavery, I shall hate it while I live." I feel those same emotions deep within my soul and believe I always will.

I'm looking forward to seeing you very soon and eating some of that Dutch cheese I am so fond of. Family members often say that you and I are much alike. If "spunk" and "sprightly" are words used to describe you, then I shall proudly be called the same.

Your Loving Granddaughter,

Fanny

brother
me that you are in
are well, Baby
so, even by his
all
a
able to
you would have
when I

Mother

McConnelsville, Ohio • October, 1833

Dearest Loving Mother,

I hope this letter finds you feeling much better. I was greatly worried upon receiving brother George's letter and hearing of your ailments. He has assured me that you are in the best of hands in tending to your needs.

The children are well. Baby Charles is growing like a weed. He is doted upon so, even by his siblings who are almost babies themselves. They keep me running in all directions. I even burnt my corncakes yesterday trying to chase down a giggling George in a wet diaper. By the time I caught him, I was unable to take it off as I had knotted it too tightly. Oh, Mother, you would have laughed yourself well at my predicament. James even chortled when I shared the story with him at supper last night, all the while brushing off blackened pieces of corncake.

My industrious young husband continues to work hard. His legal practice is growing but he insists that he would like to enter into another line of work, as traveling to courts outside of our local area is tiring, and it keeps him away from home more often than he prefers. I will end this letter with a promise that I will soon visit you and Father. Please continue to rest. James, the children, and I, all send you our love.

Your Devoted Daughter,

Fanny

Father

McConnelsville, Ohio • May, 1842

Dearest Father,

I just finished reading a newly published poem by Henry Wadsworth Longfellow titled: *A Slave's Dream*. I've been writing verse for many years now and it is my fervent hope that my own poetry might one day help send such a message about the malevolence of slavery.

Do you remember that small area of the house that you referred to as my sanctum? I would retreat there when writing until the light grew too dim for me to see. Oh, how fond my memories are of those years spent under the loving protection of you and Mother. Dear, dear Mother. How I miss her these seven years since she passed away.

Thank you for your kind words of encouragement concerning my current instruction. Mrs. Corner is a wonderful teacher, providing me with semi-weekly lessons. She admitted to being hesitant in tutoring me because I am so busy caring for my children and household duties. I believe I pleasantly surprised her as she declared she has never before listened to such recitations, even with a baby on my lap, a cradle full of children, my foot on the rocker, and my hands busy with knitting.

I remember your own efforts in legislating for public schooling when our state was newly formed. I applaud you, Father, for all your good works in that direction. Even now I am hesitant to admit that I was jealous of my brothers being able to attend college in Athens while my own schooling seemed so inadequate. I am adamant that my children will all receive a good education, regardless of their gender.

I continue to hope that your health will allow you to make the trip to McConnelsville for an extended stay at my home. The children and I enjoyed our short visit with you in the fall. You were kind to allow my inquisitive brood to continually ply you with questions about your own childhood growing up back east and your part in helping to settle the Ohio territory. I must admit that I was mesmerized as much as they were by your fascinating stories of shipbuilding, Indian wars, and even the tragic Blennerhassetts. You are a true pioneer of our young nation. I take such pride in being your daughter. I pray you stay well, Father. My thoughts are always with you. Love always.

Fanny

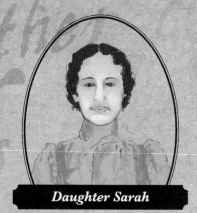

Daughter Sarah

McConnelsville, Ohio • May, 1848

My Darling Daughter Sarah,

My heart swelled with pride upon reading how well you are doing at Putnam Female Seminary. Your father chides me for making so much of this to family and close friends in letters and visits. He says that everyone knows well the abilities of his daughter and I've no need to brag.

I know that I have told you before about the history of the town of Putnam. You may take pride in knowing that it has withstood embattlement from a drunken mob that tried to stop abolitionists from speaking at Stone Academy, the first location of your fine educational institution. As your father and I have also relayed to you many times, do not wander from Putnam into the growing town of Zanesville as it is not safe for a young woman. I will write my cousin Abigail who lives close by and ask her to send a carriage for you on Sunday afternoons. I know that time from your studies is precious, but I do hope that visits with family will aid in alleviating your feeling of homesickness.

I am told that Dr. Increase Mathews of Putnam raises Merino sheep. Sadly, I report to you that the Muskingum River rose to great proportions one evening this past December and drowned over 1,000 Merino sheep on the Dana farm. Many farmers' crops in the Waterford area were destroyed as well. We pray for those in such great need at this time.

Study hard, my dearest Sarah. Be safe by staying within the boundaries of your educational establishment. Know that you are missed at home. Your brothers and sister send their love along with a bountiful number of hugs.

Always Lovingly Yours,

Mother

McConnelsville, Ohio • June, 1850

Dearest Sister Charlotte,

Please forgive me for my lapse in writing as so much has happened recently. I told you in my last leter that I have been corresponding with Lucretia Mott. She is a forthright woman who, along with Elizabeth Cady Stanton, organized the first women's rights convention in Seneca Falls, New York two years ago. Lucretia has been urging me to speak out on the issues of women's rights and abolition. With her support, as well as assistance from some local ladies, I can now proudly report that I have given my first speech regarding human rights.

This event took place in McConnelsville at the Masonic Hall. My words were brief, yet passionate for change. "I believe the words white and male should be omitted from the new Ohio Constitution." Replies from the audience were mixed as some applauded the idea while others cried out that I was brewing up trouble. I am not deterred from my course, dear sister. I shall continue to say my say.

My beloved husband James and the children are all well. I continue to count my blessings that we were able to move into our spacious home, Mount Airy, considering we have eight youngsters to raise. The ballroom also provides me with the necessary space to hold meetings concerning reform issues. I will confess that the current state of James' iron foundry business is worrisome in these economic times. He tries not to worry me about financial issues, but I do not feel he should bear the entire brunt of such concerns. We both believe in a marriage of equality, and I think it is time to remind him that this means sharing our burdens as well.

I have heard others speak of your own work to further the cause of temperance, my dear sister. I am proud of all that you do, especially in encouraging all those local young boys to take a pledge to abstain from the unhealthy use of tobacco and the scourge of strong drink. I find great comfort and pride in knowing that we are not only sisters by blood but by our zeal for eliminating grog from our society as well.

Please give my love to the family. I hope we will see each other soon.

Fanny

Elizabeth Cady Stanton

Akron, Ohio • May, 1851

Dearest Mrs. Elizabeth Cady Stanton,

Having just finished serving as president of the Ohio Women's Rights Convention in Akron, I am anxious to write you of the great success we achieved in furthering our cause. I must admit that, while honored, I did feel inexperienced to serve in this capacity. I hope I served with the dignity such a position commanded.

While the whole of the convention is worth sharing, I shall write of one speaker who left an impression upon the entire audience, male and female. That speaker was Sojourner Truth.

The pews were filled with people, many who were sneering and mocking the orators and event organizers. Ministers had spoken about God not wanting women to have equal rights. Others claimed that men had more rights and privileges because they had superior intellect. The crowd had become rowdy and Sojourner's appearance, as a six-foot tall, former slave and woman, seemed to stir them even more. "Don't let her speak, Mrs. Gage, it will ruin us."

I looked out among the crowd, hearing the hissing and vulgar words being thrown toward old Sojourner and myself. A tempest had descended upon the Akron convention and I was apprehensive about what to do next. Making my decision, I silenced the audience and proceeded to introduce Sojourner as the next speaker. Sojourner's words were powerful. I emphatically feel that her *And Ain't I a Woman* speech was integral in perhaps turning the tide of this convention toward the right of suffrage. Our cause must be built upon such accomplishments as these.

I look forward to hearing from you and hopefully meeting with you at future reform-minded events. Until then, I am your most avid admirer.

Fanny D Gage

Note: *The popular version of Sojourner Truth's "And Ain't I a Woman" speech was told by Frances Gage in 1863, twelve years after the actual event took place.*

Sister Catharine

McConnelsville, Ohio • September, 1851

Dearest Sister Catharine,

Oh, with what joy I received your letter today. It makes the distance between us seem not as far when I read of the antics of your children, hear you reminisce about our childhood, and smell the dried flowers that you drop into each envelope. I have a small area in my garden containing the Iowa flowers you so lovingly provide me with.

In writing of the local news that you always ask for, we have had many young men head west in search of their fortunes. This does not surprise me as the newspapers have been filled with news of gold strikes in California. Do you remember young George Washington Thissell? He went by G.W. He and several other local men left with Henry Seamon, Jerry Sheppard, and the Palmer brothers for the California gold fields where all the other so called forty-niners have gathered. His letters home are shared among the neighbors. I shudder when reading of the fighting amongst the men, robberies, diseases, Indian encounters, and the liberal use of whiskey. Of course, there are also tales of the buffalo hunts, expansive countryside, and hopes of finding gold that keep a multitude of young men pining to go. Many mothers, sisters, and young wives are fearful that they might lose their own men to the lure of that glittering rock.

I recently penned a poem trying to persuade the local men not to go to California. I believe my verses have fallen on deaf ears and that many more will follow the paths west, either overland or by sea. Many are passing through your fair state of Iowa and I pray they will find reason to plant their feet in the firm soil of your countryside or to return to their homes in the Buckeye State.

I am happy to hear that your neighborhood is prospering and that you are feeling less dispirited than in your last letter. Still, we were all disappointed to hear that you will not be making the trip home so that we may wrap our loving arms around you. I believe the hillsides of Ohio would give you strength. I will close by stating that not a day passes that I do not think of you. All the neighbors send their love, as you are not forgotten in our small town. Do, do write often.

Your Loving Sister,

Fanny

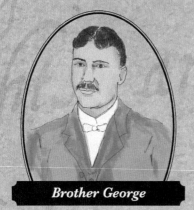

Brother George

McConnelsville, Ohio • February, 1852

Dear Brother George,

It was relayed to me in a recent letter that you have not been feeling well. I'm sorry to hear this and hope that you have sought proper medical care. Medical advances have come far from our days growing up on the family farm. Do you remember when Catharine was so ill with the flux? The doctor was called in and put blisters on her wrists by applying mustard plasters to draw out all the toxic infection. We were all worried so about her. She later confided to me that she snuck into the kitchen that evening and took some leftover chopped cabbage out of the cupboard. Covering it in strong vinegar, she quickly devoured a bowl full. The next morning she stated she woke up feeling much better. I now have to chuckle when I think of how Catharine still believes that coleslaw is a cure-all.

I have been quite busy traveling to local venues to speak on abolition, women's rights, and temperance. While I have spoken in larger cities, I find myself most comfortable in the rural areas. Still, even in the small towns, I am met with resistance. Last September I was scheduled to speak in Chesterfield, not far from McConnelsville. The other organizers and I ended up holding our meeting in a large barn because suffragists weren't welcome in the town churches or school. Oh, but it was a spirited assembly of men, women, and children who gathered at the barn to hear about equal rights, regardless of color or gender.

A recent meeting held at Mount Gilead began in a disappointing manner, as no folks had shown up and the meeting place was not well organized. I soon found some boys playing nearby and promised to pay each one 10¢ if they could bring 50 people to hear Aunt Fanny speak. It worked and the conference was a success. I guess you could state that I have to pay to say my say sometimes.

I hope to travel to Washington County soon to spread the words of reform. I will stop by to check on you and spend some time at the old homestead. I am eager to gaze upon the portrait of Father again as it hangs above your mantle. I send you heartfelt wishes for a full recovery and much love to your darling wife Emeline.

Fanny

Amelia Bloomer

St. Louis, Missouri • August, 1853

Dear Mrs. Amelia Bloomer,

I just finished reading a very stimulating article in your newspaper, *The Lily*, and was reminded that I owe you a letter. Let me say that I have thoroughly enjoyed our engaging back and forth correspondence. I also wish to thank you for the opportunities you have given me to write for *The Lily*. As you know, I continue to be a contributor to several other journals, including the *Ohio Cultivator*. This last reform-minded periodical allows me to promote the idea that the honorable housewife and mother can still be an advocate in the causes of temperance, abolition, and women's rights. I, myself, am a mother and wife. Writing letters to my readers as Aunt Fanny, I am able to impart news of activism as well as to give sensible household advice. Indeed, just as my male counterparts give sage advice on the newest farming implements, I am able to provide information on new household items that lessen the labor-laden tasks for women.

Many have asked me for my thoughts on the wearing of Turkish pants, or bloomers, as they have come to be called. I will share with you what I have formally told others. "We must own ourselves, under the law, first own our own bodies, our earnings, our genius, and our consciences; then we shall turn to the lesser matter of what shall be the garniture of the body." Between the two of us, I am envious of anyone who is able to have a piece of clothing named after her. I don't foresee any such honor in my future. Imagine having anything of fashion named after me, Fanny. I fall into fits of laughter just thinking of it.

I hope to see you at the Whole World Temperance Convention in New York City this September. I think we will become fast friends.

Your Colleague in Reform,

Fanny D. Gage

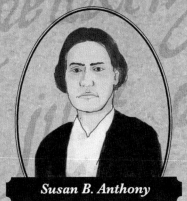
Susan B. Anthony

St. Louis, Missouri • August, 1857

My Dear Friend Susan,

I hope my letter finds you in good spirits. I have been reading news of your lectures throughout the United States and miss the time we spent together last winter sharing the message of civil rights and temperance. I am amazed at the stamina you maintain with such a heavy speaking load; some newspapers stating that Miss Susan B. Anthony delivers over 75 speeches per year, and I do not doubt this number. Although you have always been very self-conscious of public speaking, you never let it deter you from your duty. I just pray that you will not let this often arduous calling negatively affect your health.

I continue to spend much of my time discussing temperance with those who will listen. I firmly believe that drunkenness is the greatest evil in that it is harmful to families and society. Residing now in a big city like St. Louis, I constantly see the negative consequences of so many grog shops.

Between giving speeches on temperance, women's rights, and abolition in a slave state, I fear I have placed my family in some danger. I highly suspect that arsonists wanting to send me a threatening message have started three separate fires on our property. Knowing that you have dealt with violent repercussions, I look to you for advice and support. I shall stay the course, but I feel we will soon have to relocate, as my husband James' business is floundering and we are in debt. I am in great need of your encouraging words, my friend.

Let me not end on a negative note but rather say that I hope to see you at the 8th National Women's Rights Convention in New York City this coming May. Being with all my colleagues in reform is energizing and will pull me from my current poor attitude. Let's promise to make time to sit and chat over some tea on topics far from the current ills of society. I miss your company.

Fanny

Sister Mary

Parris Island, South Carolina • May, 1863

Dearest Sister Mary,

It is with a heavy heart that I write this letter to you. I have received word from my brother-in-law in Illinois that my beloved husband has passed away. My James is now gone.

Oh, that I would have been with him during this time, but I felt the need to be of some service to my country during this great Civil War. As you know, four of my own sons are serving in the Union Army, fighting for the freedom of blacks against the bondage of slavery. I felt honored indeed when given the opportunity to serve as the superintendent of Parris Island, home to over 500 newly freed slaves. Educating these liberated people on how to become self-sufficient has been the main goal of this program. I have learned so much here. In addition to organizing the facility, I have also helped with nursing, cooking, gardening, cleaning, and educating the young and old. It has been a very humbling and rewarding experience, one that I'm sure dear James would not have wanted me to miss.

I met an amazing woman while here. Her name is Clara Barton and she has been as close to the front lines of battle as many soldiers. She has taught me much about nursing and courage in the face of imminent danger. In return, I feel I have enlarged her views of what constitutes civil and moral injustice. We have become good friends and have been good company for each other in a stressful place and time. We both enjoy reading poetry and often sit in the beautiful garden I have developed here and read verses to each other. I will miss her.

I will come home for a brief respite. I want to grieve within the comfort of my family in the hills of Ohio. Let us pray that this terrible war ends soon and that all of our boys return back to the love and safety of their families. Take care dear sister.

Affectionately,

Fanny

Frederick Douglass

Lambertville, New Jersey • August, 1869

Dearest Mr. Frederick Douglass,

I begin this letter by stating that our courses are interwoven, even though quarrels over the impending passage of the 15th Amendment have split the American public's beliefs concerning the necessity of women's rights versus rights for the newly freed slaves. As you have long been aware, I strongly feel that human rights activists should be united in our quest for equality for all. We should be of one voice. Many of my fellow suffragists believe that giving black males the vote, while leaving out women, could set back the cause of suffrage.

Our fellow activist, Wendell Phillips, has long urged us to educate the blacks. Who has done this task if not northern women? Does it make sense that we give colored men the vote but refuse their teachers the same right? I have always believed that women's rights, abolition, and temperance reforms are part of the same cord. If you remove one strand, the cord is weakened. I do not believe, however, that denying black men the vote will usher in my rights as a woman any sooner. Having long fought for the freedom of slaves, I can also find hope in the creation of the 15th Amendment and the progress being made in granting citizens the right to vote, regardless of race. I pray that it is ratified.

Yours in Reform,

Fanny D Gage

Note: Women's rights organizations were divided over the creation of the 14th and 15th Amendments to the Constitution. While citizenship and the right to vote were given to blacks, these rights were granted to males only.

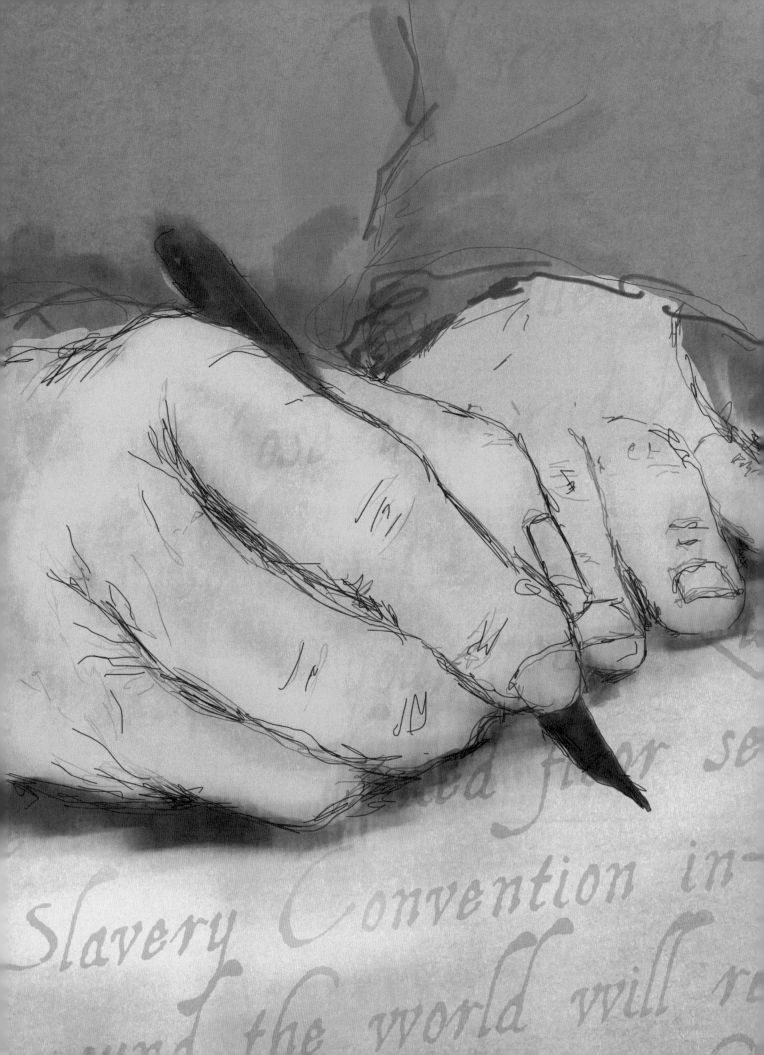

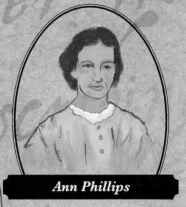

Ann Phillips

New York • February, 1872

Dearest Friend Ann,

Forgive me for not staying in touch. It has been too long since we have seen each other, although I do keep abreast of Wendell's activities through mutual friends and what I glean from the newspapers. But, how are you, dear friend? I have heard that your health has not been good in recent years.

As you know, my own poor health has precluded me from taking as active a role in our causes as I would prefer. I send letters to conventions and attend those that I am able to. Still, I have found that I had to choose another path in furthering our interest for human rights and temperance, that is, writing novels that demonstrate the destructiveness of drunken carousing and discrimination based on gender. I have been advised by my grandchildren to write a story that includes romance, heroines, and a generous dose of good and evil, and they shall read it. I am rather of a mind that the realities of everyday life are what our readers need to hear. Thus, I have written about what I know, changing names and places so that the characters are not recognized in real life.

I received a letter from my close friend, Clara Barton, last week. She too has been ill and is recuperating in England. She wrote a lengthy description of her work with the International Red Cross, describing many of the sites she visited while working in Europe. I'm sure you and Wendell visited some of those same places during your trip abroad so many years ago. Has it truly been over 30 years since you, Lucretia Mott, and many of our sisters were denied floor seats to the World's Anti-Slavery Convention in London? Suffragists from around the world will remember your often-quoted statement, "Don't shilly-shally Wendell!" How we smile when thinking of the wife of the famous orator, Wendell Phillips, encouraging her husband to speak on behalf of women seeking membership to that event. What a struggle it has been to have our voices heard and our gender recognized.

I hope you will feel better soon. Age is not kind to the body. Give my best to Wendell. I urge him to use his close connection with President Grant to remind him of the consequences of his well-reported use of ardent spirits. We need a President who models self-control.

Fanny

Son Joseph

Iowa • September, 1874

My Dear Son Joseph,

Your sister Sarah and I have arrived in Iowa. It was a very long journey, noticeably harder since my younger days and before that debilitating stroke. Still, I am thankful that we are here to visit with your brother Ambrose and my cherished sister Catharine.

As I sat on the train for what seemed like an endless journey, I was reminded of all the traveling I have done in the course of my life, most of it to further the causes of abolition, suffrage, and temperance. In the early days, it was only a few hours' journey to the local meeting places where I spoke to the country folks, my neighbors and friends. Yes, there was resistance. There always is where a worthy cause can be found. But there was camaraderie as well. Think of all that has been accomplished and yet so much to be done.

Our battle for the abolition of slavery was a success with the creation of the Emancipation Proclamation and 13th Amendment. There are still battles to be fought in that field, as prejudices are hard to die. Let us also remember the long, terrible war that you and your brothers fought so that blacks are not shackled and sold at auctions.

Our struggle for women's rights is ongoing. We have made progress but it has been slow and laborious. We are still striving for legal rights for married women, equal pay for equal work, and, of course, the vote! I will be speaking at a convention here in Iowa very soon. This work must continue.

I am extremely disappointed in the lack of headway I see concerning the issue of temperance. I have spent the last few years, while recuperating, writing novels that delve into the sinkhole that inebriation creates. Out of the three I have written, I am most pleased with the success of *Elsie Magoon*, as it was well received by the reading public. Why then have we not made progress in closing down the grog shops and liquor stores? I remember back many years ago in McConnelsville to a petition composed by temperance advocates asking the court to shut down the drinking establishments. Judge Stillwell of Muskingum County refused, stating "woman's place was in the nursery and the parlor, and that when she interfered in public affairs, or set herself up as an instructor of the courts, she was out of her sphere." How long has it been that men have been confining us to their definition of a woman's sphere?

I fear I am giving you one of my speeches. I shall stop now and begin anew tomorrow with news of your Iowa family. I'm longing to be out in the fresh air to sample some fruit that is supposed to be so sweet here. Do you know that when I was a young girl, growing up in Ohio, they used to tempt people to come to Iowa by stating the cows came home at night with legs stained red up to their knees from walking through fields of wild strawberries.

Please write me all the news and I will be sure to share it with your family here. Give hugs to everyone.

With Much Love,

Mother

Sister Catharine

Greenwich, Connecticut • September, 1884

Dearest Sister,

I got your letter yesterday but was too ill to read it then. I am feeling better today and it provided a bright spot in my morning to read news of you and your family. It is hard to believe that you are almost 78 and I am only two years behind you. We must both pass over the river soon.

In the past days I have been thinking back to our childhood. Do you remember all the cedar trees around the house? I used to swing on the vines that would hang from the tallest trees and Mother would fret that I would fall. Dear Mother. She was the most gentle of women I ever knew. Do you remember her pet fawn? I enjoyed hearing her stories about traveling over 700 miles from New England to Marietta by ox-cart and then flatboat. Still, what I enjoyed even more was being outside helping Father with the chores. I would have traded places with our brothers in a minute and left them to do the dishes with you while I tended to the animals and plowed the fields. Sister, I can still remember the day when I helped the cooper make a barrel, better than any other barrels on our property. I was called in to the house by Mother but overheard Father tell the cooper, "What a pity she was not a boy." I was ten years old when I overheard him say that. I made my mind up right then that I would not be limited by my sex. That has driven my life since.

Oh, what a life I have had. My wonderful husband James and eight children have been such a blessing to me. How I miss James and two of my boys, but my remaining are all happy and well. I have known remarkable men and women who were my equals in the cause of human rights reform. Lucretia Mott, Susan B. Anthony, Horace Greeley, Lucy Stone, Amelia Bloomer, Elizabeth Cady Stanton, ole Sojourner Truth, Wendell Phillips, William Lloyd Garrison, and dear Clara Barton. So many more that worked tirelessly. I attended countless meetings in small towns as well as conventions in the largest cities in our country. So much was done, my sister. So much remains to be done.

Give all your children and grandchildren best wishes from Aunt Fanny. Do go to Ohio if you can. I wish I could join you but I know that this life will soon come to an end. I am not suffering so please do not worry about me. God is good. I await His tender mercies.

Affectionately,

Fanny

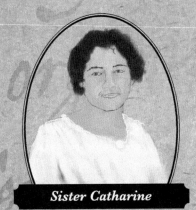

Sister Catharine

Greenwich, Connecticut • November 11, 1884

Dearest Aunt,

After four days of intense suffering, the longed for rest has come to Mother. Last night at ten o'clock, her pain increased till her tired nature could endure no longer.

"Oh! I am so tired" she gasped a short time before she passed away, crossing over the river. She has earned her rest. Hers has been a life well done.

Affectionately,

Sarah Joseph Mary

Note: All but the final three lines in this letter are exactly as written by Frances D. Gage's children to their Aunt Catharine informing her of the passing of her sister. This letter is part of the Catharine Barker Memoirs held in the Marietta College Special Collections in Marietta, Ohio.

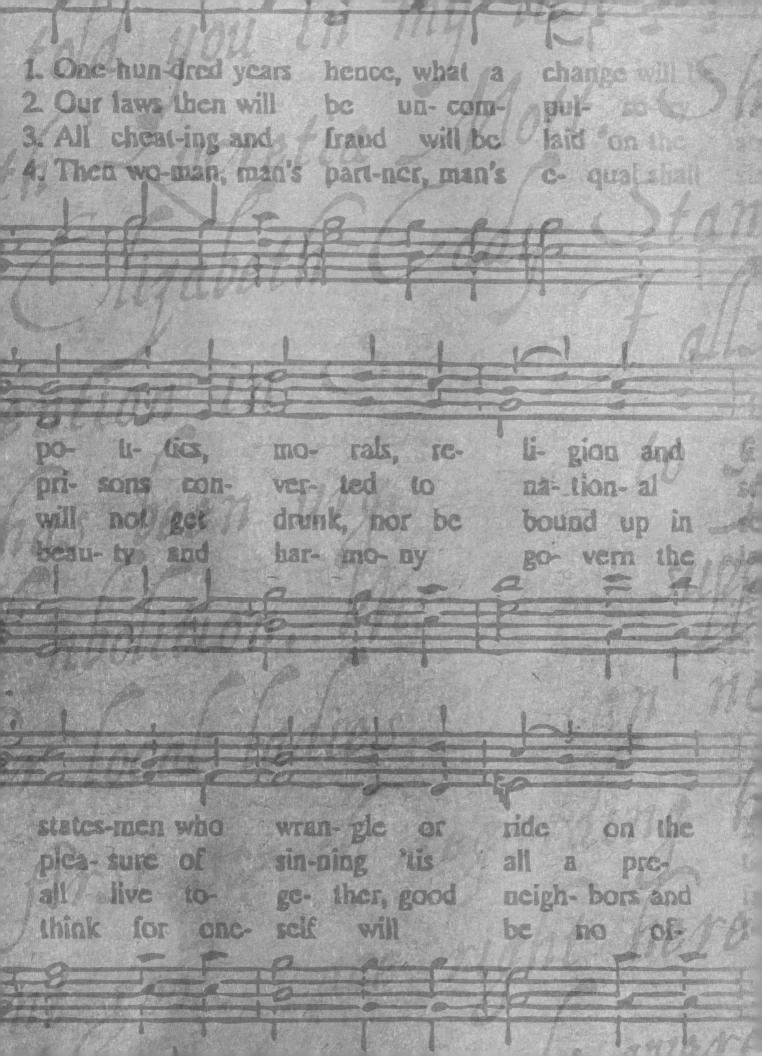

A Hundred Years Hence
Frances Dana Barker Gage
(Composed in 1852)

One hundred years hence, what a change will be made
In politics, morals, religion and trade,
In statesmen who wrangle or ride on the fence,
These things will be altered, a hundred years hence.

Our laws then will be uncompulsory rules,
Our prisons converted to national schools,
The pleasure of sinning 'tis all a pretense,
And people will find that, a hundred years hence.

All cheating and fraud will be laid on the shelf,
Men will not get drunk, nor be bound up in self,
But all live together, good neighbors and friends,
As Christian folks ought to, a hundred years hence

Then woman, man's partner, man's equal shall stand,
While beauty and harmony govern the land,
To think for oneself will be no offense,
The world will be thinking, a hundred years hence.

Oppression and war will be heard of no more
Nor blood of a slave leave his print on our shore,
Conventions will then be a useless expense,
For we'll go free-suffrage, a hundred years hence.

Instead of speech-making to satisfy wrong,
We'll all join the chorus to sing Freedom's song;
And if the Millennium is not a pretense,
We'll all be good neighbors, a hundred years hence.

Grandmother Dana

Brother Luther

Mother

Father

Daughter Sarah

Sister Charlotte

Elizabeth Cady Stanton

Sister Catharine

Brother George

Amelia Bloomer

Susan B. Anthony

Sister Mary

Frederick Douglass

Ann Phillips

Son Joseph

Cathy Mowrer

About the Author

Cathy Mowrer is an education professor at Marietta College in Marietta, Ohio. She spent many years as an elementary school teacher before receiving her Ph.D. and teaching at the college level. Cathy's pursuits lie in telling the accounts of those true heroes whose stories are not often heard. She is the author of *Young Thomas Ewing and the Coonskin Library*. *Letters from Fanny: Highlights in the Life of Frances Dana Barker Gage* is her second book.

Emily B. Hendershot

About the Illustrator

Emily Bonnette Hendershot is an artist and graphic designer born in Marietta, Ohio. She resides in her hometown with her husband Mark. She believes in communicating the beauty of God's love through art. She is the illustrator of *Young Thomas Ewing and the Coonskin Library*. *Letters from Fanny: Highlights in the Life of Frances Dana Barker Gage* is her second book.

For additional infomation regarding Frances Dana Barker Gage and Schoolmarm Books, visit www.schoolmarmbooks.com.

Bibliography

Catharine Barker Memoirs, Marietta College Library.

Foner, Philip S. ed. *Frederick Douglass on Women's Rights*. New York: DeCapo, 1992.

Frost, Elizabeth and Kathryn Cullen-DuPont. *Women's Suffrage in America: An Eyewitness History*. New York: Facts on File. 1992.

Miller, Susan Cummins, ed. *A Sweet Separate Intimacy: Women Writers of the American Frontier, 1800-1922*. Salt Lake City: The University of Utah Press.

Smith, Jeffrey E. "Frances Dana Gage: Turning the World Upside Down." *Feminist Frontiers: Women Who Shaped the Midwest*. Ed. Yvonne J. Johnson. Kirksville: Truman State University Press. 2010. 1-19.

Stanton, Elizabeth Cady, Susan B. Anthony, and Matilda Joslyn Gage, eds. *History of Woman Suffrage*. Vol 2. New York: Fowler & Wells, 1882.

Steinhagen, Carol. "The Two Lives of Frances Dana Gage." *Ohio History* 107 (Winter-Spring 1998): 22-38.

The Ohio Cultivator. Vol VIII. Columbus: M.B. Bateham. 1852. 173.

OHIO
HISTORICAL
MARKER

MOUNT AIRY MANSION

Mt. Airy Mansion, a Federal style home built in 1843, is best known as the home of Frances Dana Gage. As a prominent leader in the women's rights movement, Gage hosted many women's rights meetings in the mansion's Ball Room. In 1868, Hugh and Mary Cochran purchased the home, which remained in the family for 107 years. The Cochrans owned and operated the Cochran Tobacco Company from 1837 until 1951. The cigar manufacturer was the largest employer in Morgan County, and was recognized as the largest manufacturer of plug tobacco north of the Mason-Dixon line at the beginning of the Civil War.

THE OHIO BICENTENNIAL COMMISSION
THE INTERNATIONAL PAPER COMPANY FOUNDATION
THE OHIO HISTORICAL SOCIETY
2003   12-58

Made in the USA
Monee, IL
08 July 2021